HISTORY'S MOST INFLUENTIAL
INVENTORS

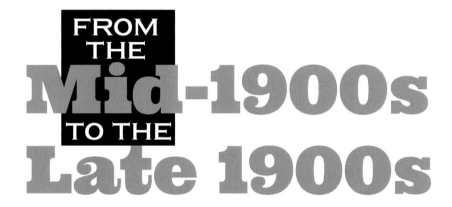

FROM THE Mid-1900s TO THE Late 1900s

Charles Stark Draper to Gertrude B. Elion

EDITED BY ROBERT CURLEY

IN ASSOCIATION WITH

ROSEN
EDUCATIONAL SERVICES

Published in 2025 by Britannica Educational Publishing
(a trademark of Encyclopædia Britannica, Inc.)
in association with Rosen Educational Services, LLC
2544 Clinton Street, Buffalo, NY 14224.

Copyright © 2025 Encyclopædia Britannica, Inc. Britannica, Encyclopædia Britannica, and the Thistle logo are registered trademarks of Encyclopædia Britannica, Inc. All rights reserved.

Rosen Educational Services materials copyright © 2025 Rosen Educational Services, LLC. All rights reserved.

Distributed exclusively by Rosen Educational Services.
For a listing of additional Britannica Educational Publishing titles, call toll free (800) 237-9932.

First Edition

Britannica Educational Publishing
Michael I. Levy: Executive Editor
Marilyn L. Barton: Senior Coordinator, Production Control
Steven Bosco: Director, Editorial Technologies
Lisa S. Braucher: Senior Producer and Data Editor
Yvette Charboneau: Senior Copy Editor
Kathy Nakamura: Manager, Media Acquisition
Robert Curley: Manager, Science and Technology

Editor: Greg Roza
Book design: Michael Flynn

Photo credits: Cover https://commons.wikimedia.org/wiki/File:Gertrude_Elion.jpg; p. 12 https://commons.wikimedia.org/wiki/File:Felix_Wankel_1960s.jpg; p. 17 https://commons.wikimedia.org/wiki/File:JohnvonNeumann-LosAlamos.gif; p. 22 https://en.wikipedia.org/wiki/File:Commodore_Grace_M._Hopper_USN_(covered).jpg; p. 24 Gordon Bell/Shutterstock.com; p. 30 https://commons.wikimedia.org/wiki/File:EdwardTeller1958_fewer_smudges.jpg; p. 35 https://commons.wikimedia.org/wiki/File:Michael_E._DeBakey.jpeg; p. 41 https://commons.wikimedia.org/wiki/File:Edwin_H._Land,_founder,_Polaroid.jpg; p. 43 https://commons.wikimedia.org/wiki/File:Dr._Virginia_Apgar_welcoming_world%27s_newest_guest._LCCN2002712240.jpg; p. 45 https://commons.wikimedia.org/wiki/File:FenderTremoloPatentDiagram.png; p. 54 https://commons.wikimedia.org/wiki/File:Wernher_von_Braun.jpg; p. 57 https://commons.wikimedia.org/wiki/File:Charles_Townes.jpg.

Cataloging-in-Publication Data

Names: Curley, Robert, 1955-.
Title: From the mid-1900s to the late 1900s: Charles Stark Draper to Gertrude B. Elion / edited by Robert Curley.
Description: New York : Britannica Educational Publishing, in Association with Rosen Educational Services, 2025. | Series: History's most influential inventors | Includes glossary and index.
Identifiers: ISBN 9781641900997 (library bound) | ISBN 9781641900980 (pbk) | ISBN 9781641901000 (ebook)
Subjects: LCSH: Inventors--Biography. | Inventions--History.
Classification: LCC T39.F766 2025 | DDC 609.2'2--dc23

Manufactured in the United States of America

CPSIA Compliance Information: Batch #CSBRIT25. For further information contact Rosen Publishing at 1-800-237-9932.

CONTENTS

Introduction 4
Charles Stark Draper 6
William P. Lear 9
Felix Wankel 11
John von Neumann 13
Chester F. Carlson 20
Grace Murray Hopper 21
Frank Whittle 23
John Mauchly and J. Presper Eckert . . 26
Edward Teller 29
Michael DeBakey 33
Willard Libby 36
Edwin Herbert Land 39
Virginia Apgar 42
Leo Fender 44
William Shockley, John Bardeen,
   and Walter Brattain 46
Wernher von Braun 51
Charles Townes 56
Gertrude B. Elion 58
Glossary 60
For More Information 61
Index 62

Introduction

"The most dangerous phrase in the language is, 'We've always done it this way.'"
—*Grace Murray Hopper (1906–1992)*

Today, life in the United States and other developed countries is about ease and convenience. Communication is global and instantaneous. Transportation can carry people across states, countries, and even entire continents in a matter of hours. Industry has been automated, providing people with plenty of time outside of work to enjoy leisure pursuits. Modern medical treatments have enabled people to stay healthy well into their eighth, ninth, or even tenth decade.

Life has been transformed over the years through the efforts of the men and women who had the brilliance, diligence, and creativity to come up with new and better ways of doing things. This book focuses on the inventions of people who lived from the mid-1900s to the late 1900s. As detailed throughout these pages, their inventions spawned many more inventions, speeding up the pace of progress even further.

The old saying, "Necessity is the mother of invention," couldn't be more true. Inventors have had a knack for recognizing a need or problem in society and then discovering a way to fill that need or solve that problem. Many inventions have clearly improved life by keeping people healthier, helping them to communicate and work more efficiently, and allowing them to travel farther.

One of the fields where invention has made the greatest strides is in medical science. This book includes the inventions of three remarkable medical pioneers: Michael DeBakey, who revolutionized cardiovascular surgery;

Virginia Apgar, who established a system for assessing the health of infants; and Gertrude B. Elion, who helped develop lifesaving medications.

Other inventions were controversial because of their potential for destruction. Edward Teller, father of the hydrogen bomb, was described by one scientist as being one of the "most thoughtful statesmen of science." However, another contemporary referred to Teller as "a danger to all that's important," and claimed that the world would have been better off without him.

Many of the inventors in this book saw great success during their lifetimes. They earned fame, recognition, and a place in history. Some, such as Willard Libby and Gertrude B. Elion, received what is thought to be the highest honor—the Nobel Prize.

This book recognizes not only the inventors whose work changed the course of human life, but also those whose ideas paved the way for future generations of inventors. Often inventors were inspired by one another.

So many inventors have made important contributions in this time period that to mention them all here would far exceed the space limitations of this book. The figures who have been included are among the greatest and most prolific inventors of all time. They were selected because their inventions have altered the course of people's lives and have left an indelible stamp on human history.

CHARLES STARK DRAPER

(b. Oct. 2, 1901, Windsor, Mo., U.S.—d. July 25, 1987, Cambridge, Mass.)

Charles Stark Draper was an American aeronautical engineer, educator, and science administrator whose laboratory at the Massachusetts Institute of Technology (MIT) was a center for the design of navigational and guidance systems for ships, airplanes, and missiles from World War II through the Cold War. Combining basic research and student training and supported by a network of corporate and military sponsors, Draper's laboratory was one of the proving grounds for post-World War II Big Science.

Draper received a B.A. in psychology from Stanford University in 1922. He then enrolled at MIT and earned a B.S. in electrochemical engineering in 1926. He remained at MIT to do graduate work in physics and soon demonstrated his precocity as both a researcher and entrepreneur. As a graduate student he became a national expert on aeronautical and meteorological research instruments. The Instruments Laboratory (I-Lab), which he founded in 1934, became a center for both academic and commercial research, a combination that was not unusual at the time. It was through the I-Lab that Draper established a relationship with the Sperry Gyroscope Company (now part of Unisys Corporation). Though they would later become competitors, Sperry provided critical support for the fledgling laboratory and jobs for Draper's graduate students. Draper also operated a consulting business that further extended his academic and industrial connections. Appointed to the MIT faculty in 1935, he was promoted to professor after receiving his Doctor of Science degree.

With the start of World War II, Draper turned to developing antiaircraft weapons. The airplane had emerged as a critical weapon of modern warfare, and fighters proved too fast and agile for traditional fire-control systems. With support from Sperry and MIT, Draper and his students designed and built the Mark 14 gyroscopic lead-computing gunsight. Based on a radical new spring mechanism, the gunsight calculated an aircraft's future position, taking into account gravity, wind, and distance. Overcoming the problems posed by the production of the sight demanded that Sperry hire Draper's students to oversee the manufacturing process, while Draper trained naval officers in the newly renamed Confidential Instruments Development Laboratory on the use of the new sight. By war's end more than 85,000 Mark 14 sights had been built and installed on American and British warships, making it by far the most popular sight of its kind used by Allied navies during World War II.

After World War II Draper's interests expanded beyond the development of antiaircraft fire-control systems for capital ships and gunsights to the development of self-contained navigation systems for aircraft and missiles. During World War II radar and other radio- and microwave-based technologies had greatly increased the ability of aircraft to navigate to their targets under various weather conditions and with an unprecedented degree of accuracy. However, these systems were vulnerable to enemy jamming and provided foes with an electromagnetic phantom to track and attack. Other methods of aerial navigation, such as celestial navigation, produced no signals but depended upon the skillful use of instruments and the cooperation of the weather. As the Soviet Union became the main enemy of the United States in the postwar period, the development of a navigation system for aircraft and missiles that did not need external referents or trained humans became a national research priority. Working first with gyroscopes insulated in a climate-controlled viscous fluid and later with accelerometers, Draper developed entirely self-contained inertial guidance systems. These machines were so precise that they could compute a vehicle's exact position from its initial position and acceleration; needing no further inputs, they were invulnerable to enemy countermeasures. The first experimental systems for aircraft, Projects FEBE and SPIRE, were tested in 1949 and 1953. Production systems were installed in aircraft and submarines beginning in 1956 and in the Polaris missile in 1960. The "black boxes" of spinning gyroscopes and integrating circuits developed by Draper and his students were eventually deployed in the Air Force's Atlas, Titan, and Minuteman missiles and the Navy's Poseidon and Trident missiles, placing them at the core of the U.S. thermonuclear arsenal during the Cold War.

Inertial guidance provided a solution to critical technical problems in Cold War nuclear strategy. Equally important to its popularity and success was Draper's training of civilian and military engineers, who learned his methods, became disciples of self-contained navigation, made his systems work in the field, and awarded the I-Lab contracts. With the creation of the Weapons System Engineering Course in 1952, Draper institutionalized one mechanism for the development of a technological intelligentsia within the armed services and made the lab a center for producing both guidance systems and the people to use them. Graduates of the program were among inertial guidance's most enthusiastic supporters and sources for Laboratory contracts, and they supervised the development of the nation's intercontinental and submarine-launched ballistic systems that used inertial systems. It was a Draper graduate, Robert Seamans, who gave the I-Lab the contract for the development of the Apollo program guidance system that successfully guided Neil Armstrong, Buzz Aldrin, and Michael Collins to the moon and back.

Students, precision machinery, personal relationships, and federal patronage in civilian and military form made Draper a towering figure in 20th-century engineering and engineering education. Ironically, at the height of his success, in the late 1960s, both he and the I-Lab became the focus of inquiry into the effects of military patronage on MIT. After much protesting by antiwar activists and internal discussion among faculty and administrators, MIT decided in 1970 to divest itself of the laboratory. It was renamed the Charles Stark Draper Laboratory, Inc., and moved off campus in 1973. For a man who was first and foremost a teacher, it was the most undeserved of fates, especially at the institute whose modern form he had done so much to shape. Nonetheless, Draper's career reflected one of the fundamental changes in 20th-century academia: the transformation of academic research into big business supported by the armed services and major corporations. In partial recognition of the scope and significance of Draper's career, the National Academy of Engineering established the Charles Stark Draper Prize in 1988 to honor "innovative engineering achievement and its reduction to practice in ways that have contributed to human welfare and freedom."

WILLIAM P. LEAR

(b. June 26, 1902, Hannibal, Mo., U.S.—d. May 14, 1978, Reno, Nev.)

William Powell Lear was a self-taught American electrical engineer and industrialist whose Lear Jet Corporation was the first mass-manufacturer of business jet aircraft in the world. Lear also developed the automobile radio, the eight-track stereo tape player for automobiles, and the miniature automatic pilot for aircraft.

The child of immigrant parents and a broken home, Lear said that at the age of 12 he had worked out a blueprint of his life, based upon profiting by inventing what people wanted. He held some 150 patents at his death.

After completing eighth grade, Lear quit school to become a mechanic and at the age of 16 joined the navy, lying about his age. During World War I, Lear studied radio and after his discharge designed the first practicable auto radio. Failing to secure the financial backing to produce the radio himself, Lear sold the radio to the Motorola Company in 1924.

In 1934 he designed a universal radio amplifier (i.e., one that would work with any radio). The Radio Corporation of America purchased the plans, giving Lear the capital he needed to expand his operations. He founded the Lear Avia Corporation in 1934 to make radio and navigational devices for aircraft. In 1939 he founded Lear, Inc. By 1939 more than half the private airplanes in the United States were using Lear radio and navigational equipment. In World War II, the company manufactured cowl-flap motors and other precision devices for Allied aircraft. After World War II, Lear, Inc., introduced a new, miniaturized autopilot that could be used on small fighter aircraft.

Between 1950 and 1962 the sales of Lear, Inc., rose to $90,000,000. New plants were added in the Midwest and on both coasts, and the company embarked on the manufacture of stereophonic sound systems and miniature communications satellites. Lear himself wanted to expand into low-priced, small jet aircraft for businessmen. When his board of directors would not approve the expenditure, Lear sold his share of the company and formed Lear Jet, Inc., Wichita, Kansas, which produced its first compact jet in 1963. The new company's jets became among the world's most popular private jet aircraft. Lear sold his interest in the corporation in 1967 and formed Lear Motors Corporation (1967–69) to produce a steam car.

FELIX WANKEL
(b. Aug. 13, 1902, Lahr, Ger.—d. Oct. 9, 1988, Lindau, W. Ger.)

German engineer Felix Wankel was the inventor of the Wankel rotary engine. The Wankel engine is radically different in structure from conventional reciprocating piston engines. Instead of pistons that move up and down in cylinders, the Wankel engine has a triangular orbiting rotor that turns in a closed chamber. Each quarter turn of the rotor completes an expansion or a compression of the gases inside the chamber, permitting the four functions characteristic of all internal-combustion engines—intake, compression, expansion, and exhaust—to be accomplished during one turn of the rotor. The only moving parts are the rotor and the output shaft. In theory, the advantages of this design include light weight, few moving parts, compactness, low initial cost, fewer repairs, and relatively smooth performance.

Wankel never earned an engineering degree and in fact never acquired a driver's license. The son of a forestry official in the Black Forest region of southern Germany, he grew up in straitened circumstances after his father was killed in World War I. As a young man, convinced that he could design a practical rotary engine (the concept was well-known but usually dismissed as unworkable), he set up a small engineering business in Heidelberg while financing himself with other jobs such as bookselling. He was briefly a member of the Nazi Party before it rose to power. During the Nazi and World War II period he settled in Lindau, on Lake Constance near the border with Switzerland, where he worked on designs for seals, unconventional rotary valves, and rotary engines for automobile

From the Mid-1900s to the Late 1900s
Charles Stark Draper to Gertrude B. Elion

Felix Wankel (1902–1988) gained fame as the inventor of an internal-combustion rotary engine.

and airplane engines. At various times he worked for the Daimler-Benz and BMW automobile companies as well as the German air force. At the end of the war his workshop was dismantled by the Allied authorities, and in 1951 he began working in Lindau with the research department of an engine manufacturer, NSU Motorenwerk AG. He completed his first design of a rotary engine for NSU in 1954, and prototype units were tested in 1957 and 1958. In 1961 Mazda, a Japanese automobile company, contracted with NSU to produce and develop the Wankel engine in Japan. Rotary-engined Mazda cars were introduced to the Japanese market in the 1960s and to the American market in 1971. Wankel established a series of his own research establishments at Lindau, where he continued to work under contract for various companies on the fundamental problems and future applications of the rotary engine. He received a number of honors from engineering societies in Germany and abroad, and in 1969 he was awarded an honorary doctorate from the Technical University of Munich. Committed all his life to antivivisectionism, Wankel in 1972 founded the annual or semiannual Felix Wankel Animal Welfare Research Award for papers and projects related to animal welfare and the cessation of experimentation on live animals.

JOHN VON NEUMANN

(b. Dec. 28, 1903, Budapest, Hung.—d. Feb. 8, 1957, Washington, D.C., U.S.)

John von Neumann (originally named János Neumann) was a Hungarian-born American mathematician. As an adult, he appended *von* to his surname; the hereditary title had been granted his father in 1913. Von Neumann grew from child prodigy to one of the world's foremost mathematicians by his mid-20s. Important work in set theory inaugurated a career that touched nearly every major branch of mathematics. Von Neumann's gift for applied mathematics took his work in directions that influenced quantum theory, automata theory, economics, and defense planning. Von Neumann pioneered game theory and, along with Alan Turing and Claude Shannon, was one of the conceptual inventors of the stored-program digital computer.

Early Life and Mathematical Career

Von Neumann grew up in an affluent, highly assimilated Jewish family. His father, Miksa Neumann (Max Neumann), was a banker, and his mother, born Margit Kann (Margaret Kann), came from a family that had prospered selling farm equipment. He earned a degree in chemical engineering (1925) from the Swiss Federal Institute in Zürich and a doctorate in mathematics (1926) from the University of Budapest.

From 1926 to 1927 von Neumann did postdoctoral work under David Hilbert at the University of Göttingen. He then took positions as a Privatdozent ("private lecturer") at the Universities of Berlin (1927–29) and Hamburg (1929–30). The work with Hilbert culminated in von Neumann's book *The Mathematical Foundations of Quantum Mechanics* (1932), in which quantum states are treated as vectors in a Hilbert space. This mathematical synthesis reconciled the seemingly contradictory quantum mechanical formulations of Erwin Schrödinger and Werner Heisenberg. Von Neumann also claimed to prove that deterministic "hidden variables" cannot underlie quantum phenomena. This influential result pleased Niels Bohr and Heisenberg and played a strong role in convincing physicists to accept the indeterminacy of quantum theory. In contrast, the result dismayed Albert Einstein, who refused to abandon his belief in determinism.

In 1928 von Neumann published "Theory of Parlor Games," a key paper in the field of game theory. The nominal inspiration was the game of poker. Game theory focuses on the element of bluffing, a feature distinct from the pure logic of chess or the probability theory of roulette. Though von Neumann knew of the earlier work of the French mathematician Émile Borel, he gave the subject mathematical substance by proving the mini-max theorem. This asserts that for every finite, two-person zero-sum game, there is a rational outcome in the sense that two perfectly logical adversaries can arrive at a mutual choice of game strategies, confident that they could not expect to do better by choosing another strategy. In games like poker, the optimal strategy incorporates a chance element. Poker players must bluff occasionally—and unpredictably—in order to avoid exploitation by a savvier player.

In 1929 von Neumann was asked to lecture on quantum theory at Princeton University. This led to an appointment as visiting professor (1930–33). He was remembered as a mediocre teacher, prone to write quickly and erase the blackboard before students could copy what he had written. In 1933 von Neumann became one of the first professors at the Institute for Advanced Study (IAS), Princeton, New Jersey. The same year, Adolf Hitler came to power in Germany, and von Neumann relinquished his German academic posts. In a much-quoted comment on the Nazi regime, von Neumann wrote, "If these boys continue for only two more years . . . they will ruin German science for a generation—at least."

Though no longer a teacher, von Neumann became a Princeton legend. It was said that he played practical jokes on Einstein, could recite verbatim books that he had read years earlier, and could edit assembly-language computer code in his head. Von Neumann's natural diplomacy helped him move easily among Princeton's intelligentsia, where he often adopted a tactful modesty. He once said he felt he had not lived up to all that had been expected of him. Never much like the stereotypical mathematician, he was known as a wit, bon vivant, and aggressive driver—his frequent auto accidents led to one Princeton intersection being dubbed "von Neumann corner."

WORLD WAR II AND AFTER

In late 1943 von Neumann began work on the Manhattan Project at the invitation of J. Robert Oppenheimer. Von Neumann was an expert in the nonlinear physics of hydrodynamics and shock waves, an expertise that he had already applied to chemical explosives in the British war effort. At Los Alamos, New Mexico, von Neumann worked on Seth Neddermeyer's implosion design for an atomic bomb. This called for a hollow sphere containing fissionable plutonium to be symmetrically imploded in order to drive the plutonium into a critical mass at the center. The implosion had to be so symmetrical that it was compared to crushing a beer can without splattering any beer. Adapting an idea proposed by James Tuck, von Neumann calculated that a "lens" of faster- and slower-burning chemical explosives could achieve the needed degree of symmetry. The Fat Man atomic bomb, dropped on the Japanese port of Nagasaki, used this design. Von Neumann participated in the selection of a Japanese target, arguing against bombing the Imperial Palace, Tokyo.

Overlapping with this work was von Neumann's magnum opus of applied math, *Theory of Games and Economic Behavior* (1944), cowritten with Princeton economist Oskar

John von Neumann

John von Neumann (1903–1957) made important contributions to the fields of mathematics and physics.

Morgenstern. Game theory had been orphaned since the 1928 publication of "Theory of Parlor Games," with neither von Neumann nor anyone else significantly developing it. The collaboration with Morgernstern burgeoned to 641 pages, the authors arguing for game theory as the "Newtonian science" underlying economic decisions. The book created a vogue for game theory among economists that has partly subsided. The theory has also had broad influence in fields ranging from evolutionary biology to defense planning.

In the postwar years, von Neumann spent increasing time as a consultant to government and industry. Starting in 1944, he contributed important ideas to the U.S. Army's hard-wired ENIAC computer, designed by J. Presper Eckert, Jr., and John W. Mauchly. Most important, von Neumann modified the ENIAC to run as a stored-program machine. He then lobbied to build an improved computer at the Institute for Advanced Study. The IAS machine, which began operating in 1951, used binary arithmetic—the ENIAC had used decimal numbers—and shared the same memory for code and data, a design that greatly facilitated the "conditional loops" at the heart of all subsequent coding. Von Neumann's publications on computer design (1945–51) created friction with Eckert and Mauchly, who sought to patent their contributions, and led to the independent construction of similar machines around the world. This established the merit of a single-processor, stored-program computer—the widespread architecture now known as a von Neumann machine.

Another important consultancy was at the RAND Corporation, a think tank charged with planning nuclear strategy for the U.S. Air Force. Von Neumann insisted on the value of game-theoretic thinking in defense policy. He supported development of the hydrogen bomb and was reported to have advocated a preventive nuclear strike to destroy the Soviet Union's nascent nuclear capability circa 1950. Despite his hawkish stance, von Neumann defended Oppenheimer against attacks on his patriotism and warned Edward Teller that his Livermore Laboratory (now the Lawrence Livermore National Laboratory) cofounders were "too reactionary." From 1954 until 1956, von Neumann served as a member of the Atomic Energy Commission and was an architect of the policy of nuclear deterrence developed by President Dwight D. Eisenhower's administration.

In his last years, von Neumann puzzled over the question of whether a machine could reproduce itself. Using an abstract model (a cellular automata), von Neumann outlined how a machine could reproduce itself from simple components. Key to this demonstration is that the machine reads its own "genetic" code, interpreting it first as instructions for constructing the machine exclusive of the code and second as data. In the second phase, the machine copies its code in order to create a completely "fertile" new machine. Conceptually, this work anticipated later discoveries in genetics.

Von Neumann was diagnosed with bone cancer in 1955. He continued to work even as his health deteriorated rapidly. In 1956 he received the Enrico Fermi Award. Von Neumann was a lifelong agnostic, but shortly before his death he converted to Roman Catholicism. With his pivotal work on quantum theory, the atomic bomb, and the computer, von Neumann likely exerted a greater influence on the modern world than any other mathematician of the 20th century.

CHESTER F. CARLSON

(b. Feb. 8, 1906, Seattle, Wash., U.S.—d. Sept. 19, 1968, New York, N.Y.)

American physicist Chester F. Carlson was the inventor of xerography (from the Greek words meaning "dry writing"), an electrostatic photocopying process that found applications ranging from office copying to reproducing out-of-print books.

By the age of 14 Carlson was supporting his invalid parents, yet he managed to earn a college degree from the California Institute of Technology, Pasadena, in 1930. After a short time spent with the Bell Telephone Company, he obtained a position with the patent department of P.R. Mallory Company, a New York electronics firm.

Plagued by the difficulty of getting copies of patent drawings and specifications, Carlson began in 1934 to look for a quick, convenient way to copy line drawings and text. Since numerous large corporations were already working on photographic or chemical copying processes, he turned to electrostatics for a solution to the problem. The basis of the process is photoconductivity, an increase in the ability of certain substances to allow an electric current to flow through them when struck by light. The chemical element selenium, for example, is a poor electrical conductor, but when light is absorbed by some of its electrons and a voltage is applied, these electrons are able to pass more freely from one atom to another. When the light is removed, their mobility falls. Xerography typically uses an aluminum drum coated with a layer of selenium. Light passed through the document to be copied, or reflected from its surface, reaches the selenium surface, onto which negatively charged particles of ink (i.e., the toner) are sprayed, forming an image of the document on the drum. A sheet of copy paper is passed close to the drum, and a positive electric charge under the sheet attracts the negatively charged ink particles, resulting in the transfer of the image to the copy paper. Heat is then momentarily applied to fuse the ink particles to the paper.

In 1938 Carlson and a research associate succeeded in making the first xerographic copy. Carlson obtained the first of many patents for the xerographic process in 1940 and for the next four years tried unsuccessfully to interest someone in developing and marketing his invention. More than 20 companies turned him down. Finally, in 1944, he persuaded Battelle Memorial Institute, Columbus, Ohio, a nonprofit industrial research organization, to undertake developmental work. In 1947 a small firm in Rochester, New York, the Haloid Company (later the Xerox Corporation), obtained the commercial rights to xerography, and 11 years later Xerox introduced its first office copier. Carlson's royalty rights and stock in Xerox Corporation made him a multimillionaire.

GRACE MURRAY HOPPER

(b. Dec. 9, 1906, New York, N.Y., U.S. — d. Jan. 1, 1992, Arlington, Va.)

Grace Murray Hopper (née Grace Brewster Murray) an American mathematician and rear admiral in the U.S. Navy, was a pioneer in developing computer technology, helping to devise UNIVAC I, the first commercial electronic computer, and naval applications for COBOL (*c*ommon-*b*usiness-*o*riented *l*anguage).

After graduating from Vassar College (B.A., 1928), Hooper attended Yale University (M.A., 1930; Ph.D., 1934). She taught mathematics at Vassar College, Poughkeepsie, New York, from 1931 to 1943 before joining the U.S. Naval Reserve. She became a lieutenant and was assigned to the Bureau of Ordnance's Computation

From the Mid-1900s to the Late 1900s
Charles Stark Draper to Gertrude B. Elion

Grace Hopper (1906–1992) was a trailblazing computer scientist.

Project at Harvard University (1944), where she worked on Mark I, the first large-scale automatic calculator and a precursor of electronic computers. She remained at Harvard as a civilian research fellow while maintaining her naval career as a reservist. After a moth infiltrated the circuits of Mark I, she coined the term *bug* to refer to unexplained computer failures.

In 1949 Hopper joined the Eckert-Mauchly Computer Corp., where she designed an improved compiler, which translated a programmer's instructions into computer codes. She remained with the firm when it was taken over by Remington Rand (1951) and by Sperry Rand Corp. (1955). In 1957 her division developed Flow-Matic, the first English-language data-processing compiler. She retired from the navy with the rank of commander in 1966, but she was recalled to active duty the following year to help standardize the navy's computer languages. At the age of 79, she was the oldest officer on active U.S. naval duty when she retired again in 1986. She was elected a fellow of the Institute of Electrical and Electronic Engineers (1962), was named the first computer science Man of the Year by the Data Processing Management Association (1969), and was awarded the National Medal of Technology (1991).

FRANK WHITTLE

(b. June 1, 1907, Coventry, Warwickshire, Eng.—d. August 8, 1996, Columbia, Md., U.S.)

Frank Whittle was an English aviation engineer and pilot who invented the jet engine.

The son of a mechanic, Whittle entered the Royal Air Force (RAF) as a boy apprentice and soon qualified as a pilot at the RAF College in Cranwell. He was posted to a fighter squadron in 1928 and served as a test pilot in 1931–32. He then

FROM THE MID-1900S TO THE LATE 1900S
CHARLES STARK DRAPER TO GERTRUDE B. ELION

Frank Whittle (1907–1996) was the inventor of the jet engine.

pursued further studies at the RAF engineering school and at the University of Cambridge (1934–37). Early in his career Whittle recognized the potential demand for an aircraft that would be able to fly at great speed and height, and he first put forth his vision of jet propulsion in 1928, in his senior thesis at the RAF College. The young officer's ideas were ridiculed by the Air Ministry as impractical, however, and attracted support from neither the government nor private industry.

Whittle obtained his first patent for a turbo-jet engine in 1930, and in 1936 he joined with associates to found a company called Power Jets, Ltd. He tested his first jet engine on the ground in 1937. This event is customarily regarded as the invention of the jet engine, but the first operational jet engine was designed in Germany by Hans Pabst von Ohain and powered the first jet-aircraft flight on August 27, 1939. The outbreak of World War II finally spurred the British government into supporting Whittle's development work. A jet engine of his invention was fitted to a specially built Gloster E.28/39 airframe, and the plane's maiden flight took place on May 15, 1941. The British government took over Power Jets, Ltd., in 1944, by which time Britain's Gloster Meteor jet aircraft were in service with the RAF, intercepting German V-1 rockets.

Whittle retired from the RAF in 1948 with the rank of air commodore, and that same year he was knighted. The British government eventually atoned for their earlier neglect by granting him a tax-free gift of £100,000. He was awarded the Order of Merit in 1986. In 1977 he became a research professor at the U.S. Naval Academy in Annapolis, Maryland. His book *Jet: The Story of a Pioneer* was published in 1953.

JOHN MAUCHLY AND J. PRESPER ECKERT

respectively, (b. Aug. 30, 1907, Cincinnati, Ohio, U.S.—d. Jan. 8, 1980, Ambler, Pa.); (b. April 9, 1919, Philadelphia, Pa., U.S.—d. June 3, 1995, Bryn Mawr, Pa.)

During World War II, U.S. government funding went to a project led by John Mauchly, J. Presper Eckert, and their colleagues at the Moore School of Electrical Engineering at the University of Pennsylvania. Their objective was an all-electronic computer, and work began in early 1943 on the Electronic Numerical Integrator and Computer (ENIAC). The next year, mathematician John von Neumann—already on full-time leave from the Institute for Advanced Studies in Princeton, New Jersey, for various government research projects (including the Manhattan Project)—began frequent consultations with the group.

Completed by February 1946, ENIAC was something less than the dream of a universal computer. Designed for the specific purpose of computing values for artillery range tables, it lacked some features that would have made it a more generally useful machine. For instance, it used plugboards for communicating instructions to the machine. This had the advantage that, once the instructions were thus "programmed," the machine ran at electronic speed. The disadvantage was that it took days to rewire the machine for each new problem. This was such a liability that only with some generosity could ENIAC be called programmable. Still, it was the most powerful calculating device built to date and the first programmable general-purpose electronic digital computer.

ENIAC was also enormous. It occupied the 50-by-30-foot (15 by 9 m) basement of the Moore School, where its 40 panels were arranged, U-shaped, along three walls.

Each of the units was about 2 feet wide by 2 feet deep by 8 feet high (0.6 m by 0.6 m by 2.4 m). With approximately 18,000 vacuum tubes, 70,000 resistors, 10,000 capacitors, 6,000 switches, and 1,500 relays, it was easily the most complex electronic system ever built. A portion of the machine is on exhibit at the Smithsonian Institution in Washington, D.C.

John Mauchly

After completing his education, John William Mauchly entered the teaching profession, eventually becoming an associate professor of electrical engineering at the University of Pennsylvania, Philadelphia. During World War II Mauchly and Eckert, a graduate engineer, were asked to devise ways to accelerate the recomputation of artillery firing tables for the U.S. Army. They accordingly proposed the construction of a general-purpose digital computer that would handle data in coded form; by 1946 they completed ENIAC, a huge machine containing more than 18,000 vacuum tubes. ENIAC was first used by the U.S. Army at its Aberdeen Proving Ground in Maryland in 1947 for ballistics tests.

The following year Mauchly and Eckert formed a computer-manufacturing firm, and in 1949 they announced the Binary Automatic Computer (BINAC), which used magnetic tape instead of punched cards. In 1950 the Eckert–Mauchly Computer Corporation was acquired by Remington Rand, Inc. (later Sperry Rand Corporation), Mauchly becoming director of special projects. The third computer after BINAC was the Universal Automatic Computer (UNIVAC I), specially designed to handle business data. Mauchly continued his work in the computer field, winning many honors. He served as president (1959–65) and chairman of the board (1965–69) of Mauchly

Associates, Inc., and as president of Dynatrend, Inc. (1968–80) and of Marketrend, Inc. (1970–80).

J. Presper Eckert

John Presper Eckert, Jr., was educated at the Moore School of Electrical Engineering at the University of Pennsylvania, Philadelphia (B.S., 1941; M.S., 1943), where he and his professor, Mauchly, made several valuable improvements in computing equipment. In 1946 the pair fulfilled a government contract to build a digital computer, which they called ENIAC. In primitive form, ENIAC contained virtually all the circuitry used in present-day high-speed digital computers. It was used by the U.S. Army for military calculations.

In 1948 Eckert and Mauchly established a computer-manufacturing firm; a year later, they introduced BINAC, which stored information on magnetic tape rather than on punched cards. Designed to handle business data, UNIVAC I, Eckert and Mauchly's third model, found many uses in commerce and may be said to have started the computer boom. Between 1948 and 1966 Eckert received 85 patents, mostly for electronic inventions.

Eckert remained in executive positions at his company when it was acquired by Remington Rand, Inc., in 1950 and when that firm was, in 1955, merged into the Sperry Rand Corp. (later Unisys Corp.). Eckert was elected to the National Academy of Engineering in 1967 and was awarded the National Medal of Science in 1969.

EDWARD TELLER

(b. Jan. 15, 1908, Budapest, Hung., Austria-Hung. — d. Sept. 9, 2003, Stanford, Calif., U.S.)

Edward Teller was a Hungarian-born American nuclear physicist who participated in the production of the first atomic bomb (1945) and who led the development of the world's first thermonuclear weapon, the hydrogen bomb.

Teller, born Ede Teller, was from a family of prosperous Hungarian Jews. After attending schools in Budapest, he earned a degree in chemical engineering at the Institute of Technology in Karlsruhe, Germany. He then went to Munich and Leipzig to earn a Ph.D. in physical chemistry (1930). His doctoral thesis, on the hydrogen molecular ion, helped lay the foundation for a theory of molecular orbitals that remains widely accepted today. As a student in Munich, Teller fell under a moving streetcar and lost his right foot, which was replaced with an artificial one.

During the years of the Weimar Republic, Teller was absorbed with atomic physics, first studying under Niels Bohr in Copenhagen and then teaching at the University of Göttingen (1931–33). In 1935 Teller and his bride, Augusta Harkanyi, went to the United States, where he taught at George Washington University in Washington, D.C. Together with his colleague George Gamow, he established new rules for classifying the ways subatomic particles can escape the nucleus during radioactive decay. Following Bohr's stunning report on the fission of the uranium atom in 1939 and inspired by the words of President Franklin D. Roosevelt, who had called for scientists to act to defend the United States against Nazism, Teller resolved to devote his energies to developing nuclear weapons.

By 1941 Teller had taken out U.S. citizenship and joined

From the Mid-1900s to the Late 1900s
Charles Stark Draper to Gertrude B. Elion

Edward Teller (1908–2003) became known as "the father of the H-bomb" for his work developing the first thermonuclear weapon, the hydrogen bomb.

Enrico Fermi's team at the University of Chicago in the epochal experiment to produce the first self-sustaining nuclear chain reaction. Teller then accepted an invitation from the University of California at Berkeley to work on theoretical studies on the atomic bomb with J. Robert Oppenheimer; and when Oppenheimer set up the secret Los Alamos Scientific Laboratory in New Mexico in 1943, Teller was among the first men recruited. Although the Los Alamos assignment was to build a fission bomb, Teller digressed more and more from the main line of research to continue his own inquiries into a potentially much more powerful thermonuclear hydrogen fusion bomb. At war's end he wanted the U.S. government's nuclear weapons development priorities shifted to the hydrogen bomb. Hiroshima, however, had had a profound effect on Oppenheimer and other Manhattan Project scientists, and few desired to continue in nuclear weapons research.

Teller accepted a position with the Institute for Nuclear Studies at the University of Chicago in 1946 but returned to Los Alamos as a consultant for extended periods. The Soviet Union's explosion of an atomic bomb in 1949 made him more determined that the United States have a hydrogen bomb, but the Atomic Energy Commission's general advisory committee, which was headed by Oppenheimer, voted against a crash program to develop one. The debate was settled by the confession of the British atomic scientist Klaus Fuchs that he had been spying for the Soviet Union since 1942. Fuchs had known of the American interest in a hydrogen bomb and had passed along early American data on it to the Soviets. In response, President Harry Truman ordered the go-ahead on the weapon, and Teller labored on at Los Alamos to make it a reality.

Teller and his colleagues at Los Alamos made little

actual progress in designing a workable thermonuclear device until early in 1951, when the physicist Stanislaw Marcin Ulam proposed to use the mechanical shock of an atomic bomb to compress a second fissile core and make it explode; the resulting high density would make the burning of the second core's thermonuclear fuel much more efficient. Teller in response suggested that radiation, rather than mechanical shock, from the atomic bomb's explosion be used to compress and ignite the thermonuclear second core. Together these new ideas provided a firm basis for a fusion weapon, and a device using the Teller-Ulam configuration, as it is now known, was successfully tested at Enewetak atoll in the Pacific on November 1, 1952; it yielded an explosion equivalent to 10 million tons (10 megatons) of TNT.

Teller was subsequently credited with developing the world's first thermonuclear weapon, and he became known in the United States as "the father of the H-bomb." Ulam's key role in conceiving the bomb design did not emerge from classified government documents and other sources until nearly three decades after the event. Still, Teller's stubborn pursuit of the weapon in the face of skepticism, and even hostility, from many of his peers played a major role in the bomb's development.

At the U.S. government hearings held in 1954 to determine whether Oppenheimer was a security risk, Teller's testimony was decidedly unsympathetic to his former chief. "I would feel personally more secure," he told the inquiry board, "if public matters would rest in other hands." After the hearings' end, Oppenheimer's security clearance was revoked, and his career as a science administrator was at an end. Although Teller's testimony was by no means the decisive factor in this outcome, many prominent American nuclear physicists never forgave him for what they viewed as his betrayal of Oppenheimer.

Teller was instrumental in the creation of the United States' second nuclear weapons laboratory, the Lawrence Livermore Laboratory, in Livermore, California, in 1952. For almost the next four decades it was the United States' chief factory for making thermonuclear weapons. Teller was associate director of Livermore from 1954 to 1958 and from 1960 to 1975, and he was its director in 1958–60. Concurrently he was professor of physics at the University of California at Berkeley from 1953 to 1960 and was professor-at-large there until 1970.

A staunch anticommunist, Teller devoted much time in the 1960s to his crusade to keep the United States ahead of the Soviet Union in nuclear arms. He opposed the 1963 Nuclear Test Ban Treaty, which banned nuclear weapons testing in the atmosphere, and he was a champion of Project Plowshare, an unsuccessful federal government program to find peaceful uses for atomic explosives. In the 1970s Teller remained a prominent government adviser on nuclear weapons policy, and in 1982–83 he was a major influence in President Ronald Reagan's proposal of the Strategic Defense Initiative, an attempt to create a defense system against nuclear attacks by the Soviet Union. In 2003 Teller was awarded the Presidential Medal of Freedom.

MICHAEL DEBAKEY

(b. Sept. 7, 1908, Lake Charles, La., U.S.—d. July 11, 2008, Houston, Texas)

Michael Ellis DeBakey was an American cardiovascular surgeon, educator, international medical statesman, and pioneer in surgical procedures for treatment of defects and diseases of the cardiovascular system.

In 1932 DeBakey devised the "roller pump," an essential component of the heart-lung machine that permitted open-heart surgery. He also developed an efficient method of correcting aortic aneurysms by grafting frozen blood vessels to replace diseased vessels. By 1953 DeBakey had developed a technique of using plastic tubing (Dacron) instead of arterial homographs to replace diseased vessels. In 1953 he performed the first successful carotid endarterectomy for stroke, in 1964 the first successful coronary artery bypass, and in 1966 the first successful implantation of a ventricular assist device.

DeBakey received his B.S. (1930), M.D. (1932), and M.S. (1935) degrees from Tulane University School of Medicine in New Orleans. After volunteering for military service during World War II, his work with the U.S. Surgeon General's office led to the development of mobile army surgical hospitals (MASH units) and the Department of Veterans Affairs (VA) hospital research system. In 1948 he became professor of surgery and chairman of the department of surgery at Baylor College of Medicine in Houston, where he later served as president (1969–79) and then as chancellor (1979–96).

DeBakey received numerous national and international awards, including the American Medical Association Distinguished Service Award (1959), the Albert Lasker Award for Clinical Research (1963, corecipient), the Eleanor Roosevelt Humanities Award (1969), the Presidential Medal of Freedom with Distinction (1969), the U.S.S.R. Academy of Sciences 50th Anniversary Jubilee Medal (1973), and the Presidential National Medal of Science (1987). He received more than 50 honorary degrees from universities throughout the world. In 1992 he was introduced into the Academy of Athens, a society of scholars generally restricted to Greeks who have made

Michael DeBakey

Michael DeBakey (1908–2008) was a cardiovascular surgeon whose innovations paved the way for open-heart surgery and other lifesaving procedures.

significant contributions to the arts, sciences, or literature. He edited the *Yearbook of Surgery* (1958–70), was the founding editor of the *Journal of Vascular Surgery*, and served on many medical editorial boards. Among his more than 1,600 professional and lay publications is the *The New Living Heart* (1997). DeBakey later received the Denton A. Cooley Cardiovascular Surgical Society's lifetime achievement award (2007) and was bestowed with the highest and most distinguished civilian award given by the U.S. Congress, the Congressional Gold Medal of Honor (2008).

WILLARD LIBBY

(b. Dec. 17, 1908, Grand Valley, Colo., U.S.—d. Sept. 8, 1980, Los Angeles, Calif.)

Willard Frank Libby was an American chemist whose technique of carbon-14 (or radiocarbon) dating provided an extremely valuable tool for archaeologists, anthropologists, and earth scientists. For this development he was honored with the Nobel Prize for Chemistry in 1960.

Libby, the son of farmer Ora Edward Libby and his wife, Eva May (née Rivers), attended the University of California at Berkeley, where he received a bachelor's degree (1931) and a doctorate (1933). After graduation, he joined the faculty at Berkeley, where he rose through the ranks from instructor (1933) to assistant professor (1938) to associate professor (1945). In 1940 he married Leonor Hickey, by whom he had twin daughters. In 1966 he was divorced and married Leona Woods Marshall, a staff member at the RAND Corporation of Santa Monica, California.

In 1941 Libby received a Guggenheim fellowship to

work at Princeton University in New Jersey, but his work was interrupted by the entry of the United States into World War II. He was sent on leave to the Columbia War Research Division of Columbia University in New York City, where he worked with Nobel chemistry laureate Harold C. Urey until 1945. Libby became professor of chemistry at the Institute for Nuclear Studies (now the Enrico Fermi Institute for Nuclear Studies) and the department of chemistry at the University of Chicago (1945–59). He was appointed by Pres. Dwight D. Eisenhower to the U.S. Atomic Energy Commission (1955–59). From 1959 Libby was a professor of chemistry at the University of California, Los Angeles, and director of its Institute of Geophysics and Planetary Physics (from 1962) until his death. He was the recipient of numerous honors, awards, and honorary degrees.

During the late 1950s, Libby and physicist Edward Teller, both committed to the Cold War and both prominent advocates of nuclear weapons testing, opposed Nobel chemistry and peace laureate Linus Pauling's petition for a ban on nuclear weapons. To prove the survivability of nuclear war, Libby built a fallout shelter at his house, an event that was widely publicized. The shelter and house burned down several weeks later, however, which caused physicist and nuclear testing critic Leo Szilard to joke, "This proves not only that there is a God but that he has a sense of humor."

While associated with the Manhattan Project (1941–45), Libby helped develop a method for separating uranium isotopes by gaseous diffusion, an essential step in the creation of the atomic bomb. In 1946 he showed that cosmic rays in the upper atmosphere produce traces of tritium, the heaviest isotope of hydrogen, which can be used as a tracer for atmospheric water. By measuring tritium concentrations, he developed a method for dating well water and wine, as well as for measuring circulation patterns of water and the mixing of ocean waters.

Because it had been known since 1939 that cosmic rays create showers of neutrons on striking atoms in the atmosphere, and because the atmosphere contains about 78 percent nitrogen, which absorbs neutrons to decay into the radioactive isotope carbon-14, Libby concluded that traces of carbon-14 should always exist in atmospheric carbon dioxide. Also, because carbon dioxide is continuously absorbed by plants and becomes part of their tissues, plants should contain traces of carbon-14. Since animals consume plants, animals should likewise contain traces of carbon-14. After a plant or other organism dies, no additional carbon-14 should be incorporated into its tissues, while that which is already present should decay at a constant rate. The half-life of carbon-14 was determined by its codiscoverer, chemist Martin D. Kamen, to be 5,730 years, which, compared with the age of the Earth, is a short time but one long enough for the production and decay of carbon-14 to reach equilibrium. In his Nobel presentation speech, Swedish chemist Arne Westgren summarized Libby's method: "Because the activity of the carbon atoms decreases at a known rate, it should be possible, by measuring the remaining activity, to determine the time elapsed since death, if this occurred during the period between approximately 500 and 30,000 years ago."

Libby verified the accuracy of his method by applying it to samples of fir and redwood trees whose ages had already been found by counting their annual rings and to artifacts, such as wood from the funerary boat of Pharaoh Sesostris III, whose ages were already known. By measuring the radioactivity of plant and animal material obtained globally from the North Pole to the South Pole, he showed that the carbon-14 produced by cosmic-ray bombardment varied little with latitude. On March 4, 1947, Libby and his students obtained the first age determination using the carbon-14 dating technique. He also dated linen wrappings from the Dead Sea Scrolls, bread from Pompeii buried in the eruption of Vesuvius (79 CE), charcoal from a Stonehenge campsite, and corncobs from a New Mexico cave, and he showed that the last North American ice age ended about 10,000 years ago, not 25,000 years ago as previously believed by geologists. The most publicized and controversial case of radiocarbon dating is probably that of the Shroud of Turin, which believers claim once covered the body of Jesus Christ but which Libby's method applied by others shows to be from a period between 1260 and 1390. In nominating Libby for the Nobel Prize, one scientist stated, "Seldom has a single discovery in chemistry had such an impact on the thinking in so many fields of human endeavor. Seldom has a single discovery generated such wide public interest."

EDWIN HERBERT LAND

(b. May 7, 1909, Bridgeport, Conn., U.S.—d. March 1, 1991, Cambridge, Mass.)

Edwin Herbert Land was an American inventor and physicist whose one-step process for developing and printing photographs culminated in a revolution in photography unparalleled since the advent of roll film.

While a student at Harvard University, Land became interested in polarized light, i.e., light in which all rays are aligned in the same plane. He took a leave of absence, and, after intensive study and experimentation, succeeded (1932) in aligning submicroscopic crystals of iodoquinine sulfate and embedding them in a sheet of plastic. The resulting polarizer, for which he envisioned numerous uses and which he dubbed Polaroid J sheet, was a tremendous advance. It allowed the use of almost any size of polarizer and significantly reduced the cost.

With George Wheelwright III, a Harvard physics instructor, Land founded the Land-Wheelwright Laboratories, Boston, in 1932. He developed and, in 1936, began to use numerous types of Polaroid material in sunglasses and other optical devices. Polaroid was later used in camera filters and other optical equipment.

Land founded the Polaroid Corporation in 1937. Four years later he developed a widely used, three-dimensional motion-picture process based on polarized light. During World War II he applied the polarizing principle to various types of military equipment.

Land began work on an instantaneous developing film after the war. In 1947 he demonstrated a camera (known as the Polaroid Land Camera) that produced a finished print in 60 seconds. The Land photographic process soon found numerous commercial, military, and scientific applications. Many innovations were made in the following years, including the development of a color process. Land's Polaroid Land cameras, which were able to produce developed photographs within one minute after the exposure, became some of the most popular cameras in the world.

Land's interest in light and color resulted in a new theory of color perception. In a series of experiments he revealed certain conflicts in the classical theory of color perception. He found that the color perceived is not dependent on the relative amounts of blue, green, and red light entering the eye; he proposed that at least three independent image-forming mechanisms, which he called

Edwin Herbert Land

Edwin Land (1909–1991) was the inventor of the Polaroid camera.

retinexes, are sensitive to different colors and work in conjunction to indicate the color seen.

Land received more than 500 patents for his innovations in light and plastics. In 1980 he retired as chief executive officer of Polaroid but remained active in the field of light and color research by working with the Rowland Institute of Science, a nonprofit center supported by the Rowland Foundation, Inc., a corporation that Land founded in 1960. Under Land's direction, Rowland researchers discovered that perception of light and color is regulated essentially by the brain, rather than through a spectrum system in the retina of the eye, as was previously believed.

VIRGINIA APGAR
(b. June 7, 1909, Westfield, N.J., U.S.—d. Aug. 7, 1974, New York, N.Y.)

Virginia Apgar, an American physician, anesthesiologist, and medical researcher, developed the Apgar Score System, a method of evaluating an infant shortly after birth to assess its well-being and to determine if any immediate medical intervention is required.

Apgar graduated from Mount Holyoke College in 1929 and from the Columbia University College of Physicians and Surgeons in 1933. After an internship at Presbyterian Hospital, New York City, she held residencies in the relatively new specialty of anesthesiology at the University of Wisconsin and then at Bellevue Hospital, New York City, in 1935–37. In 1937 she became the first female board-certified anesthesiologist. The first professor of anesthesiology at the College of Physicians and Surgeons (1949–59), she was also the first female physician to attain the rank of full professor there. Additionally, from 1938 she was director of the

Virginia Apgar

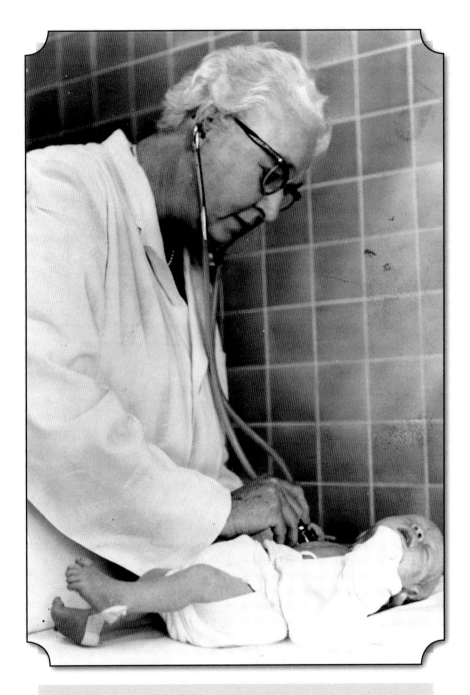

Virginia Apgar (1909–1974) developed a system for providing medical care to newborn babies.

department of anesthesiology at Columbia-Presbyterian Medical Center.

An interest in obstetric procedure, and particularly in the treatment of the newborn, led her to develop a simple system for quickly evaluating the condition and viability of newly delivered infants. As finally presented in 1952, the Apgar Score System relies on five simple observations to be made by delivery room personnel (nurses or interns) of the infant within one minute of birth and—depending on the results of the first observation—periodically thereafter. The Apgar Score System soon came into general use throughout the United States and several other countries.

In 1959 Apgar left Columbia and took a degree in public health from Johns Hopkins University. She headed the division of congenital malformations at the National Foundation-March of Dimes from 1959–67. She was promoted to director of basic research at the National Foundation (1967–72), and she later became senior vice president for medical affairs (1973–74). She cowrote the book *Is My Baby All Right?* (1972) with Joan Beck.

LEO FENDER

(b. Aug. 10, 1909, Anaheim, Calif., U.S.—d. March 21, 1991, Fullerton, Calif.)

Clarence Leo Fender was an American inventor and manufacturer of electronic musical instruments.

Together with George Fullerton, Fender developed the first mass-produced solid-body electric guitar, in 1948. Called the Fender Broadcaster (renamed the Telecaster in 1950), it was produced under the auspices of the Fender Electric Instruments Company, which Fender had formed in 1946. In 1951 the Fender Precision Bass, the world's first electric bass guitar, was unveiled, and in 1954 the Fender

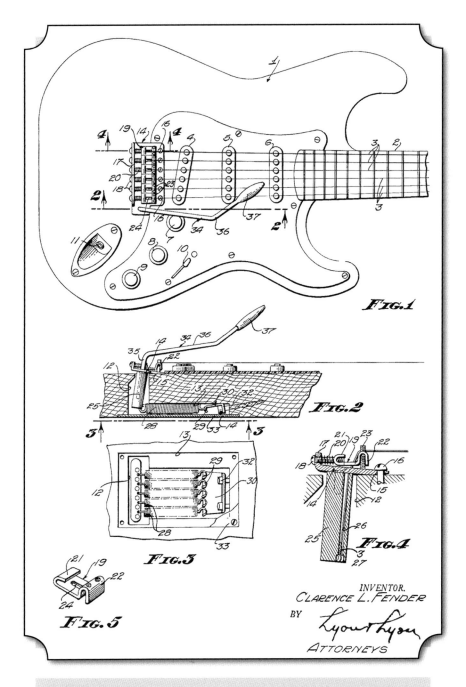

Diagrams of Clarence Fender's tremolo system were included in his 1954 application for a patent.

Stratocaster was put on the market. More stylish and technically improved than the Telecaster, the Stratocaster was the first guitar to feature three electric pickups (instead of two) and the tremolo arm used for vibrato effects. Its clean, sharp sound earned it a loyal following among guitarists, rivaled only by that of Gibson's eponymous Les Paul, and it became the signature instrument of Jeff Beck, Eric Clapton, Jimi Hendrix, and others.

Fender, who never learned to play the instrument he revolutionized, sold his manufacturing and distribution companies to CBS Corporation in 1965, a concession to his failing health. When his physical condition improved a few years later, he returned to the company as a design consultant and continued to indulge his inventive and entrepreneurial inclinations well into the 1980s.

WILLIAM SHOCKLEY, JOHN BARDEEN, AND WALTER BRATTAIN

respectively, (b. Feb. 13, 1910, London, Eng.—d. Aug. 12, 1989, Palo Alto, Calif., U.S.); (b. May 23, 1908, Madison, Wis., U.S.—d. Jan. 30, 1991, Boston, Mass.); (b. Feb. 10, 1902, Amoy, China—d. Oct. 13, 1987, Seattle, Wash., U.S.)

Electron tubes are bulky and fragile, and they consume large amounts of power to heat their cathode filaments and generate streams of electrons; also, they often burn out after several thousand hours of operation. Electromechanical switches, or relays, are slow and can become stuck in the on or off position. For applications requiring thousands of tubes or switches, such as the nationwide telephone systems developing around the world in the 1940s and the first electronic digital computers, this meant constant vigilance was needed to minimize the inevitable breakdowns.

An alternative was found in semiconductors, materials

such as silicon or germanium whose electrical conductivity lies midway between that of insulators such as glass and conductors such as aluminum. The conductive properties of semiconductors can be controlled by "doping" them with select impurities, and a few visionaries had seen the potential of such devices for telecommunications and computers. Executives at Bell Telephone Laboratories, for instance, recognized that semiconductors might lead to solid-state alternatives to the electron-tube amplifiers and electromechanical switches employed throughout the nationwide Bell telephone system. With the close of World War II, Bell Labs created a new solid-state research group headed by solid-state physicist William B. Shockley. Shockley suggested that silicon and germanium semiconductors could be used to make a field-effect amplifier. He reasoned that an electric field from a third electrode could increase the conductivity of a sliver of semiconductor material just beneath it and thereby allow usable current to flow through the sliver. But attempts to fabricate such a device by Walter H. Brattain, an experimental physicist already working at Bell Labs, and others in Shockley's group failed. The following March, John Bardeen, a theoretical physicist whom Shockley had hired for his group, offered a possible explanation. Perhaps electrons drawn to the semiconductor surface by the electric field were blocking the penetration of this field into the bulk material, thereby preventing it from influencing the conductivity.

Working closely together, Bardeen and Brattain invented the first successful semiconductor amplifier, called the point-contact transistor, on December 16, 1947. Their weird-looking device had not one but two closely spaced metal wires jabbing into the surface of a semiconductor—in this case, germanium. The input signal on one of these wires (the emitter) boosted the conductivity of the germanium beneath both of them, thus modulating the output signal on the other wire (the collector). Observers present at a demonstration of this device the following week could hear amplified voices in the earphones that it powered. Shockley, not to be outdone by members of his own group, conceived yet another way to fabricate a semiconductor amplifier the very next month, on January 23, 1948. His junction transistor was basically a three-layer sandwich of germanium or silicon in which the adjacent layers would be doped with different impurities to induce distinct electrical characteristics.

The name *transistor*, a combination of *transfer* and *resistor*, was coined for these devices in May 1948 by Bell Labs electrical engineer John Robinson Pierce, who was also a science-fiction author in his spare time. A month later Bell Labs announced the revolutionary invention in a press conference held at its New York City headquarters, heralding Bardeen, Brattain, and Shockley as the three coinventors of the transistor. The three were awarded the 1956 Nobel Prize for Physics for their invention, which ushered in the age of microminiature electronics.

WILLIAM SHOCKLEY

William Bradford Shockley studied physics at the California Institute of Technology (B.S., 1932) and at Harvard University (Ph.D., 1936). He joined the technical staff of Bell Labs in 1936 and there began experiments with semiconductors that ultimately led to the invention and development of the transistor. During World War II, he served as director of research for the Antisubmarine Warfare Operations Research Group of the U.S. Navy.

After the war, Shockley returned to Bell Labs as director of its research program on solid-state physics. Working with Bardeen and Brattain, he resumed his attempts to use semiconductors as amplifiers and controllers of electronic signals. The three men invented the point-contact transistor in 1947 and a more effective device, the junction transistor, in 1948. Shockley was deputy director of the Weapons Systems Evaluation Group of the Department of Defense in 1954–55. He joined Beckman Instruments, Inc., to establish the Shockley Semiconductor Laboratory in 1955. In 1958 he became lecturer at Stanford University, California, and in 1963 he became the first Poniatoff professor of engineering science there (emeritus, 1974). He wrote *Electrons and Holes in Semiconductors* (1950).

During the late 1960s Shockley became a figure of some controversy because of his widely debated views on the intellectual differences between races. He held that standardized intelligence tests reflect a genetic factor in intellectual capacity and that tests for IQ (intelligence quotient) reveal that Blacks are inferior to whites. He further concluded that the higher rate of reproduction among Blacks had a retrogressive effect on evolution.

John Bardeen

Two-time Nobelist John Bardeen earned bachelor's and master's degrees in electrical engineering from the University of Wisconsin, Madison and obtained his doctorate in 1936 in mathematical physics from Princeton University. A staff member of the University of Minnesota, Minnesota, from 1938 to 1941, he served as principal physicist at the U.S. Naval Ordnance Laboratory in Washington, D.C., during World War II.

After the war Bardeen joined (1945) Bell Labs in Murray Hill, New Jersey, where he, Brattain, and Shockley conducted research on the electron-conducting properties of semiconductors. On December 23, 1947, they unveiled the transistor, which ushered in the electronic revolution. The transistor replaced the larger and bulkier vacuum tube and provided the technology for miniaturizing the electronic switches and other components needed in the construction of computers. Bardeen's role in the invention of the transistor brought him his first Nobel Prize for Physics in 1956.

In the early 1950s Bardeen resumed research he had begun in the 1930s on superconductivity, and his investigations provided a theoretical explanation of the disappearance of electrical resistance in materials at temperatures close to absolute zero. The BCS theory of superconductivity (from the initials of Bardeen, Leon N. Cooper, and John R. Schrieffer) was first advanced in 1957 and became the basis for all later theoretical work in superconductivity. In 1972, with Cooper and Schrieffer, Bardeen was awarded his second Nobel Prize for Physics, for development of the theory of superconductivity. Bardeen was also the author of a theory explaining certain properties of semiconductors. He served as a professor of electrical engineering and physics at the University of Illinois, Urbana-Champaign, from 1951 to 1975.

WALTER BRATTAIN

Walter Houser Brattain earned a Ph.D. from the University of Minnesota, and in 1929 he became a research physicist for Bell Labs. His chief field of research involved the surface properties of solids, particularly the atomic structure of a material at the surface, which usually differs from its atomic structure in the interior. He, Shockley, and Bardeen invented the transistor in 1947. After leaving Bell Labs in 1967, Brattain served as adjunct professor at Whitman College, Walla Walla, Washington (1967–72), then was designated overseer emeritus. He was granted a number of patents and wrote many articles on solid-state physics.

WERNHER VON BRAUN

(b. March 23, 1912, Wirsitz, Ger.—d. June 16, 1977, Alexandria, Va., U.S.)

Wernher von Braun was a German engineer who played a prominent role in all aspects of rocketry and space exploration, first in Germany and, after World War II, in the United States.

Early Life

Braun was born into a prosperous aristocratic family. His mother encouraged young Wernher's curiosity by giving him a telescope upon his confirmation in the Lutheran church. Braun's early interest in astronomy and the realm of space never left him thereafter. In 1920 his family moved to the seat of government in Berlin. He did not do well in school, particularly in physics and mathematics. A turning point in his life occurred in 1925 when he acquired a copy of *Die Rakete zu den Planetenräumen* ("The Rocket into Interplanetary Space") by a rocket pioneer, Hermann Oberth. Frustrated by his inability to understand the mathematics, he applied himself at school until he led his class.

In the spring of 1930, while enrolled in the Berlin Institute of Technology, Braun joined the German Society for Space Travel. In his spare time he assisted Oberth in liquid-fueled rocket motor tests. In 1932 he was graduated from the Technical Institute with a B.S. degree in mechanical engineering and entered Berlin University.

By the fall of 1932 the rocket society was experiencing grave financial difficulties. At that time Captain Walter R.

Dornberger (later major general) was in charge of solid-fuel rocket research and development in the Ordnance Department of Germany's 100,000-man armed forces, the Reichswehr. He recognized the military potential of liquid-fueled rockets and the ability of Braun. Dornberger arranged a research grant from the Ordnance Department for Braun, who then did research at a small development station that was set up adjacent to Dornberger's existing solid-fuel rocket test facility at the Kummersdorf Army Proving Grounds near Berlin. Two years later Braun received a Ph.D. in physics from the University of Berlin. His thesis, which, for reasons of military security, bore the nondescript title "About Combustion Tests," contained the theoretical investigation and developmental experiments on 300- and 660-pound-thrust rocket engines.

By December 1934 Braun's group, which then included one additional engineer and three mechanics, had successfully launched two rockets that rose vertically to more than 1.5 miles (2.4 km). But by this time there was no longer a German rocket society; rocket tests had been forbidden by decree, and the only way open to such research was through the military forces.

Since the test grounds near Berlin had become too small, a large military development facility was erected at the village of Peenemünde in northeastern Germany on the Baltic Sea, with Dornberger as the military commander and Braun as the technical director. Liquid-fueled rocket aircraft and jet-assisted takeoffs were successfully demonstrated, and the long-range ballistic missile A-4 and the supersonic anti-aircraft missile Wasserfall were developed. The A-4 was designated by the Propaganda Ministry as V-2, meaning Vengeance Weapon 2. By 1944 the level of technology of the rockets and missiles being tested at Peenemünde was many years ahead of that available in any other country.

Work in the United States

Braun always recognized the value of the work of U.S. rocket pioneer Robert H. Goddard. "Until 1936," said Braun, "Goddard was ahead of us all." At the end of World War II, Braun, his younger brother Magnus, Dornberger, and the entire German rocket development team surrendered to U.S. troops. Within a few months Braun and about 100 members of his group were at the U.S. Army Ordnance Corps test site at White Sands, New Mexico, where they tested, assembled, and supervised the launching of captured V-2s for high-altitude research purposes. Developmental studies were made of advanced ramjet and rocket missiles. At the end of the war the United States had entered the field of guided missiles with practically no previous experience. The technical competence of Braun's group was outstanding. "After all," he said, "if we are good, it's because we've had 15 more years of experience in making mistakes and learning from them!"

Moving to Huntsville, Alabama, in 1952, Braun became technical director (later chief) of the U.S. Army ballistic-weapon program. Under his leadership, the Redstone, Jupiter-C, Juno, and Pershing missiles were developed. In 1955 he became a U.S. citizen and, characteristically, accepted citizenship wholeheartedly. During the 1950s Braun became a national and international focal point for the promotion of space flight. He was the author or coauthor of popular articles and books and made addresses on the subject.

In 1954 a secret army–navy project to launch an Earth satellite, Project Orbiter, was thwarted. The situation was changed by the launching of Sputnik 1 by the Soviet Union

From the Mid-1900s to the Late 1900s
Charles Stark Draper to Gertrude B. Elion

Wernher von Braun (1912–1977) was a celebrated rocket developer.

on October 4, 1957, followed by Sputnik 2 on November 3. Given leave to proceed on November 8, Braun and his army group launched the first U.S. satellite, Explorer 1, on January 31, 1958.

After the National Aeronautics and Space Administration (NASA) was formed to carry out the U.S. space program, Braun and his organization were transferred from the army to that agency. As director of the NASA George C. Marshall Space Flight Center in Huntsville, Braun led the development of the large space launch vehicles, Saturn I, IB, and V. The engineering success of each of the Saturn class of space boosters, which contained millions of individual parts, remains unparalleled in rocket history. Each was launched successfully and on time and met safe performance requirements.

In March 1970 Braun was transferred to NASA headquarters in Washington as deputy associate administrator for planning. He resigned from the agency in 1972 to become vice president at Fairchild Industries, Inc., an aerospace company. In 1975 he founded the National Space Institute, a private organization whose objective was to gain public support and understanding of space activities.

In attempting to justify his involvement in the development of the German V-2 rocket, Braun stated that patriotic motives outweighed whatever qualms he had about the moral implications of his nation's policies under Hitler. He also emphasized the innate impartiality of scientific research, which in itself has no moral dimensions until its products are put to use by the larger society. During his later career Braun received numerous high awards from U.S. government agencies and from professional societies in the United States and other countries.

CHARLES TOWNES

(b. July 28, 1915, Greenville, S.C., U.S.—d. January 27, 2015, Oakland, Calif., U.S.)

American physicist Charles Hard Townes was a joint winner with the Soviet physicists Aleksandr M. Prokhorov and Nikolay G. Basov of the Nobel Prize for Physics in 1964 for his role in the invention of the maser and the laser.

Townes studied at Furman University (B.A., B.S., 1935), Duke University (M.A., 1937), and the California Institute of Technology (Ph.D., 1939). In 1939 he joined the technical staff of Bell Telephone Laboratories, Inc., where he worked until 1948, when he joined the faculty of Columbia University. Three years later he conceived the idea of using ammonia molecules to amplify microwave radiation. In December 1953 Townes and two students demonstrated a working device that focused "excited" molecules in a resonant microwave cavity, where they emitted a pure microwave frequency. Townes named the device a maser, an acronym for "microwave amplification by stimulated emission of radiation." (At this time Prokhorov and Basov of the P.N. Lebedev Physical Institute in Moscow independently described the theory of maser operation.)

An intense burst of maser research followed in the mid-1950s, but masers found only a limited range of applications as low-noise microwave amplifiers and atomic clocks. In 1957 Townes proposed to his brother-in-law and former postdoctoral student at Columbia University, Arthur L. Schawlow (then at Bell Labs), that they try to extend maser action to the much shorter wavelengths of infrared or visible light. Townes also had discussions with a graduate student at Columbia University, Gordon Gould, who quickly developed his own laser

Charles Townes (1915–2015) is often credited as the inventor of the laser.

ideas. Townes and Schawlow published their ideas for an "optical maser" in a seminal paper in the December 15, 1958, issue of *Physical Review*. Meanwhile, Gould coined the word *laser* and wrote a patent application. Whether Townes or Gould should be credited as the "inventor" of the laser thus became a matter of intense debate and led to years of litigation. Eventually, Gould received a series of four patents starting in 1977 that earned him millions of dollars in royalties.

From 1959 to 1961 Townes served as vice president and director of research of the Institute for Defense Analyses, Washington, D.C. He then was appointed provost and professor of physics at Massachusetts Institute of Technology, Cambridge. In 1967 he became a professor at the University of California, Berkeley, where he initiated a program of radio and infrared astronomy leading to the discovery of complex molecules (ammonia and water) in the interstellar medium. He became professor emeritus in 1986.

GERTRUDE B. ELION

(b. Jan. 23, 1918, New York, N.Y., U.S.—d. Feb. 21, 1999, Chapel Hill, N.C.)

Gertrude Belle Elion was an American pharmacologist who, along with George H. Hitchings and Sir James W. Black, received the Nobel Prize for Physiology or Medicine in 1988 for their development of drugs used to treat several major diseases.

Elion was the daughter of immigrants. She graduated from Hunter College in New York City with a degree in biochemistry in 1937. Unable to obtain a graduate research position because she was a woman, she found work as a lab assistant at the New York Hospital School of Nursing

(1937), an assistant organic chemist at the Denver Chemical Manufacturing Company (1938–39), a chemistry and physics teacher in New York City high schools (1940–42), and a research chemist at Johnson & Johnson (1943–44). During this time she also took classes at New York University (M.S., 1941). Unable to devote herself to full-time studies, Elion never received a Ph.D.

In 1944 Elion joined the Burroughs Wellcome Laboratories (later part of Glaxo Wellcome; today known as GlaxoSmithKline). There she was first the assistant and then the colleague of Hitchings, with whom she worked for the next four decades. Elion and Hitchings developed an array of new drugs that were effective against leukemia, autoimmune disorders, urinary-tract infections, gout, malaria, and viral herpes. Their success was due primarily to their innovative research methods, which marked a radical departure from the trial-and-error approach taken by previous pharmacologists. Elion and Hitchings pointedly examined the difference between the biochemistry of normal human cells and those of cancer cells, bacteria, viruses, and other pathogens (disease-causing agents). They then used this information to formulate drugs that could kill or inhibit the reproduction of a particular pathogen, leaving the human host's normal cells undamaged. The two researchers' new emphasis on understanding basic biochemical and physiological processes enabled them to eliminate much guesswork and wasted effort typical previously in developing new therapeutic drugs.

Though Elion officially retired in 1983, she helped oversee the development of azidothymidine (AZT), the first drug used in the treatment of AIDS. In 1991 she was awarded a National Medal of Science and was inducted into the National Women's Hall of Fame.

Glossary

aeronautics: The science of flight and airplanes.

anesthesiologist: Physician specializing in the administration of anesthetics.

antivivisectionism: Opposition to dissecting or cutting into a live body.

cathode: The source of electrons in an electrical device.

determinism: Philosophical doctrine in which all events are inevitable consequences of previous conditions and not the result of free will.

emeritus: Retaining a title after honorably retiring from duties.

hydrodynamics: The study of fluids in motion.

isotope: One of two or more atoms with the same atomic number (number of protons in the nucleus) but with different atomic weights (numbers of neutrons in the nucleus).

patent: Rights given to a person by the government to make, use, or sell an invention.

quantum theory: The study of reactions between matter and radiation.

radiocarbon dating: Determining the age of organic objects by measuring the radioactivity of their carbon content.

roulette: A game of chance.

superconductivity: A property of some materials in which their electrical resistance goes to zero and they can carry electrical current with no energy loss.

thermonuclear: Involving the fusion of atomic nuclei at high temperatures.

transistor: An electronic device that can transform weak electrical signals into strong ones, acting as an amplifier.

For More Information

BOOKS

Gifford, Clive. 100 *Things to Know About Inventions*. Mission Viejo, CA: Happy Yak, 2021.

Montillo, Roseanne. *Atomic Women: The Untold Stories of the Scientists Who Helped Create the Nuclear Bomb*. New York, NY: Little, Brown and Company, 2020.

Uhl, Xina M., and Christy Marx. *Grace Hopper: Computer Pioneer*. New York, NY: Rosen Publishing Group, 2020.

Uhl, Xina M., and Melanie Ann Apel. *Virginia Apgar: Groundbreaking Doctor*. New York, NY: Rosen Publishing Group, 2020.

WEBSITES

American Chemical Society: Edwin Land and Polaroid Photography
www.acs.org/education/whatischemistry/landmarks/land-instant-photography.html
This article discusses Edwin Land's landmark invention of instant photography.

History Learning Site: Inventions 1900 to 1990
www.historylearningsite.co.uk/inventions-and-discoveries-of-the-twentieth-century/inventions-1900-to-1990/
Check out this timeline of 20th century inventions.

National Geographic: Cold War Facts and Information
www.nationalgeographic.com/culture/article/cold-war
Read more about the history of the Cold War, which sparked many inventions.

The Nobel Prize: Gertrude B. Elion
www.nobelprize.org/prizes/medicine/1988/elion/biographical/
This site offers a brief autobiography written by Gertrude B. Elion at the time she was awarded the Nobel Prize.

Index

aircraft, 6–10, 13, 23–25
anesthesiology, 42–44
Apgar Score System, 42–44
atomic bombs, 16, 19, 29–33, 37
automobiles, 13

Bell Telephone Laboratories, 47–50, 56

carbon-14 dating, 36–39
Cold War, 6, 8, 37
computers, 14, 18–19, 21–23, 26–28, 46

Einstein, Albert, 15–16

game theory, 14–16, 18
gyroscopes, 6–8

hydrogen bombs, 18, 29–32

jet engines, 23–25

lasers, 56–58
Los Alamos Scientific Laboratory, 16, 30–32

Manhattan Project, 16, 26, 31, 37
masers, 56–58
medicine, 33–36, 42–44, 58–59
missiles, 6–8, 52–53
musical instruments, 44–46

NASA, 55
navigation systems, 6–8
Nazis, 11, 15, 29
Nobel Prize, 36–39, 48–50, 56, 58
nuclear weapons, 16, 18–19, 28–33

Oppenheimer, J. Robert, 16, 19, 31–33

patents, 10, 20–21, 28, 42, 51, 58, 45

pharmacology, 58–59
photography, 39–42
Polaroid photography, 40–42

quantum theory, 14–15, 19

radios, 9–10
rockets, 25, 51–55
rotary engines, 11

satellites, 53–54
Soviet Union, 7, 19, 31, 33, 53
space exploration, 8, 51, 53, 55
submarines, 8, 48
surgery, 33–36

telecommunications, 47
telephones, 46, 47
thermonuclear weapons, 29, 32–33
transistors, 48–50

women inventors, 21–23, 42–44, 58–59
World War I, 10–11

World War II, 6–7, 10–13, 16, 25–27, 35, 37, 40, 47–49, 51–52

xerography, 20–21